CRAWLY SCHOOL FOR BUGS

Poems by David L. Harrison

Illustrated by Julie Bayless

POEMS TO DRIVE YOU BUGGY

WORD∫ONG

AN IMPRINT OF HIGHLIGHTS

Honesdale, Pennsylvania

For information about permission to
reproduce selections from this book,
contact permissions@highlights.com.

WordSong
An Imprint of Highlights
815 Church Street
Honesdale, Pennsylvania 18431
Printed in China

ISBN: 978-1-62979-204-0
Library of Congress Control Number: 2017942354

First edition

Designed by Barbara Grzeslo
The text of this book is set in News Gothic.
The illustrations are done in watercolor,
ink, colored pencil, and digital media.

10 9 8 7 6 5 4 3 2 1

To Cheryl Harness,
treasured friend and creative genius
who always knows what happened
this day in history
—DLH

For Doug, who inspires me to fly, leap, and dig deep
—JB

Crawly School

Welcome
    hummers,
        tweeters,
            SINGERS,
   diggers,
       LEAPERS,
          creepers,
             wingers.

Come by air,
hop or crawl—
Crawly School
welcomes all!

Our School Motto

Crawly bugs are always cool.

We obey the Golden Rule—

NEVER EAT A FRIEND AT SCHOOL!

Crawly! Crawly! Crawly!

Tick Lesson:
The Problem with People

Teacher says it's not a rumor,
people have no sense of humor.
She says they hate it when we bite,
hide our heads and dig in tight.
She says they're good with evil squeezers,
quick to grab us with their tweezers.
She says if someone yells, "I gottum!"
prepare to have a painful bottom.

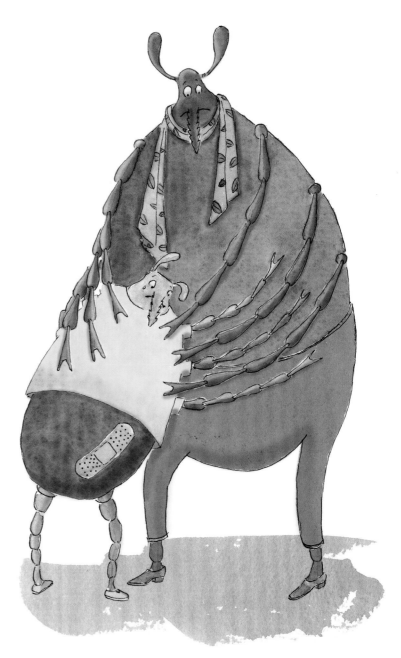

What's Left of Termite Class

Today at school
we ate some snacks—
pointers, posters,
pictures, plaques,
pansy petals,
ballpoint pens,
puppet piggies,
play-dough hens,
purple plastic
pansy pots,
pencils, paste,
and paper dots—

We ate the walls
and foundation,
hungry for more
alliteration.

IDENTIFY YOUR PLANKS

Stink Bug Class

"Smell that smell?"
complained a kid.
At first we didn't,
then we did!
We got a whiff
and it was awful.
A stink like that
should be unlawful!

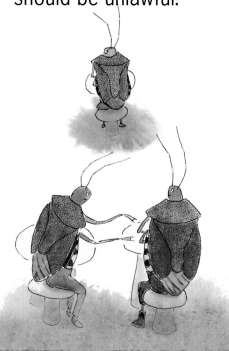

We grabbed our noses.
Gagged,
"Pee-yoo!"
"What could it be?"
No one knew.

Every kid
began to fuss.
Then someone
pointed out—
"It's us."

Horsefly Grade Card:
Doesn't Play Well with Others

In my heart
I know, of course,
it isn't nice
to bite a horse.

They've tried to teach me
gentleness,
but after school,
as you can guess,

Even though
I feel remorse,
I must go out
and bite a horse.

Camouflage Class

"It pays to hide,"
our teacher said.
"Change your color,
blend,
play dead.
Look like
something else instead.
Sit so still
you disappear."

One kid went
too far,
we fear.

He's gone
without a trace
behind him.

We've looked
and looked,
but we can't
find him.

Mr. D.

Mr. D.
will stop
to mop the halls.

He'll straighten up
our messes
during recesses

Or scrub a sink
or hose
and clean up stink.

He likes to be
our janitor
when duty calls,

But most of the time
he's busy
making

dung balls.

Crawly Hero of the Year
(A Wasp in Her Own Words)

A dog **this big**
came sniffing around,
making an urgent
whining sound.

He hiked one leg,
and we all knew
exactly what
he meant to do!

We were doomed,
and I could see
this was a job
that called for me!

We won't see him again
this year.
I zapped that dog
right on his rear.

Cricket Lessons:
How to be Annoying in 4 Easy Steps

First—
    find a private nook,
        a secret place they'll never look.
        Underneath the bed's the worst.
        They're always going to look there
          first.
        Go down the hall beneath the stair.
        No one's going to find you there.

Second—
    do not make a peep
        until you're sure they're all asleep.
        Here is what it's going to take
        to make their eyelids snap awake—
        one soft chirp to make it seem
        they might have heard you in a
          dream.

Third—
    a few more chirps and then
        their search for you will now begin.
        Armed with brooms and spray they'll
            sneak,
    lift and pry and poke and peek.

Fourth—
    you do it all once more.
        Hide and chirp again—
    next door.

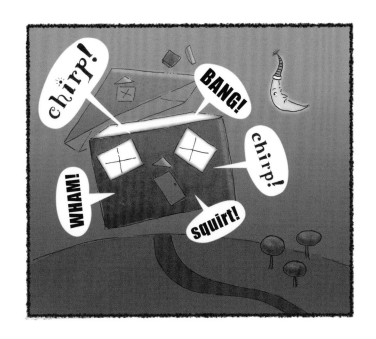

Private Thoughts of a Praying Mantis in the Lunchroom

Tender
buggy
treats . . .
Sigh.

I could catch them
off guard.

I promised
not
to eat
at school,

But, boy, oh boy,
is this
hard!

My Life as a Lightning Bug

They call me
Sparky,
Dim Bulb,
Blinky,
On-and-Offy,
Flicker,
Winky . . .

But when the lights
go off again,
guess who
everyone
loves
then?

Our School Nurse

She always takes some blood,
which always makes it worse,
which always makes us sorry
a mosquito is our nurse.

Know Your Mats

Teacher says
a mat's a trap.
We need to know
the score.

You think it's there
to welcome bugs?
That isn't what
it's for.

Pretty soon
they'll bring a broom
and s-l-o-w-l-y
lift the mat.

Before we know
what whopped us,
teacher says
we'll be
Kersplat!

On the Playground

What We Learn in Bird Class

Don't try to run.
Don't blink an eye.
Don't flick a tongue.
Don't try to fly.
Don't twitch a leg.
Don't shift a wing.
Don't turn your head.
Don't move a thing!

Beware the bird!
Beware the eye!
Beware the beak
or bug, bye-bye.

Aphid Math

Mama has fifty
babies a week.

Her babies
have fifty more.

If you add
all the babies
from all of her babies,
what do you get
for a score?

If you add all the aunties
and even the grannies,
there must be a zillion
or more!

We love all our sisters
and brothers
and cousins—

But counting us all?
What a bore!

Hiding from Spiders: Run, Don't Count!

Teacher says,
"Don't count their eyes.
If you count eight—

it's too late."

Today's Lesson in Grasshopper Class

People *eat* us!
I feel sick!
It's disgusting!
Gross! Ick!
Roasted, steamed,
spread with mustard,
honeyed, creamed,
ground in custard,
buttered, boiled,
sautéed, dried,
skewered, oiled,
floured, fried—
It's fine to eat
the farmer's crop
but eating US
has got to stop!!

Cicada Call

Final call—
"Ahree! Ahree!"

Class is over,
bugs are free!

Bugs are taking off
in flights.

Last bug out
turn off the lights!